20TH CENTURY *music*

20s & 30s

BETWEEN THE WARS

Please visit our web site at: www.garethstevens.com
For a free color catalog describing Gareth Stevens Publishing's list of high-quality books
and multimedia programs, call 1-800-542-2595 or fax your request to (414) 332-3567.

Library of Congress Cataloging-in-Publication Data

Hayes, Malcolm.
    20s & 30s: between the wars / by Malcolm Hayes.
       p. cm. — (20th century music)
    Includes bibliographical references and index.
    Summary: Discusses the influence of people and events worldwide after World War I
which led to a renewal of folk and national music, neo-classicism, the popularization of jazz,
and political repression of musicians under communist and fascist regimes.
    ISBN 0-8368-3032-6 (lib. bdg.)
    1. Music—20th century—History and criticism—Juvenile literature. [1. Music—20th
century—History and criticism.] I. Title: 20s and 30s. II. Title. III. 20th century music.
ML3928.H355   2002
780'.9'04—dc21   2001054223

This North American edition first published in 2002 by
Gareth Stevens Publishing
A World Almanac Education Group Company
330 West Olive Street, Suite 100
Milwaukee, WI 53212 USA

Original edition © 2001 by David West Children's Books. First published in Great Britain
in 2001 by Heinemann Library, Halley Court, Jordan Hill, Oxford OX2 8EJ, a division of Reed
Educational and Professional Publishing Limited. This U.S. edition © 2002 by Gareth Stevens, Inc.
Additional end matter © 2002 by Gareth Stevens, Inc.

Designer: Rob Shone
Editor: James Pickering
Picture Research: Carrie Haines

Gareth Stevens Editor: Alan Wachtel

Photo Credits:
Abbreviations: (t) top, (m) middle, (b) bottom, (l) left, (r) right

AKG London: pages 5(tr), 12(l), 15(br), 17(t), 21(br), 23(br), 24(tr).
Archivo Manuel de Falla/Lebrecht Collection: page 19(mr).
The Art Archive: pages 6(b), 25(b).
The Bridgeman Art Library: cover (br), pages 6(tr), 6-7, 26-27.
The Britten Estate: page 26(r).
Mary Evans Picture Library: pages 4(r), 5(br), 17(b), 28(r).
Hulton Getty: pages 15(ml), 22(tr), 26(bl), 29(tl).
The Kobal Collection: pages 21(bl, mr), 22(bl), 25(t).
Lebrecht Collection: cover (m), pages 4-5(t, b), 7(tl), 8(all), 9(both), 10(t), 11(all), 13(t, m),
    14, 15(t, bl), 16(both), 17(m), 18(both), 19(tl), 20(tr), 22-23, 23(mr), 24(b), 24-25,
    27(both), 28(b), 29(m, b).
Redferns: page 20(l).
TL/Lebrecht Collection: page 19(b).
Kurt Weill Foundation/Lebrecht Collection: pages 3, 12(r), 13(b).

Printed in the United States of America

1 2 3 4 5 6 7 8 9 06 05 04 03 02

20TH CENTURY *music*

20s & 30s

BETWEEN THE WARS

Malcolm Hayes

Gareth Stevens Publishing
A WORLD ALMANAC EDUCATION GROUP COMPANY

CONTENTS

Joe "King" Oliver (1885–1938), (back row, behind drummer) was one of jazz's great cornet players. His Creole Jazz Band was a hit in Chicago and made some brilliant recordings.

In 1933, Adolf Hitler's National Socialist Party was elected to power in Germany. Also known as the Nazi Party, Hitler and his followers transformed the country into a militaristic, racist, and fascist state.

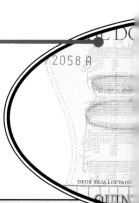

After spending some time in Paris in the 1920s, Brazilian composer Heitor Villa-Lobos returned to Brazil to write music and to teach.

REBUILDING, RETHINKING

After World War I (1914–1918), the world was a different place. The great empires of Europe had fallen apart into exhausted and squabbling nation states, troubled by mass unemployment and political instability. The Wall Street stock market crash of 1929 threw the United States into a deep economic depression. But the "Roaring Twenties" and the 1930s were also about having a good time. Jazz captured the mood perfectly, and it swept through America and Europe.

Composers, like everyone else, were trying to move forward into a strange, new age. Different composers responded in different ways. Arnold Schoenberg explored controversial twelve-tone, or "serial," music. Stravinsky's neoclassical works were inspired by the great music of the past. The genius of George Gershwin brought the influence of jazz into classical concert halls.

This illustration is from an early recording of Turandot, the last opera written by Giacomo Puccini. This opera is still perfomed regularly around the world.

TWELVE-TONE MUSIC

The chromatic scale of Western music has twelve notes. For centuries, composers had used these notes in the traditional way. In his early atonal compositions, however, Arnold Schoenberg (1874–1951) discovered that his music's harmonic language didn't seem to work in traditional terms anymore. So he came up with the "twelve-tone method," also known as "serialism."

Although Schoenberg, pictured here in a self-portrait, created a new kind of music, he was not merely rebelling against Austro-German musical tradition. He was trying to extend that tradition.

COUNTING FROM ONE TO TWELVE

Twelve-tone music was an idea waiting to happen. In America, Charles Ives (1874–1954) had already experimented with it. Schoenberg developed his own music's chromatic harmony and counterpoint into a method of composing that resulted in lean and sharply focused music.

The State Opera, formerly known as the Court Opera, is a proud landmark in Vienna. Schoenberg described Austria's music-loving capital city as "Our loathed and beloved Vienna." The Viennese generally did not like his music.

For Webern, nature was a primary inspiration. He was an enthusiastic and expert mountain climber. He also collected alpine flowers, which he took home to Vienna and planted in his garden.

COMPOSING NOTES IN ROWS

The main idea in Schoenberg's twelve-tone method is to keep a sense of harmonic and melodic balance by composing music using note-rows, or "series," that include all twelve notes, not repeating a note until all the others have already been sounded. A twelve-tone series can be used backward, upside down (inverted), or both. The notes in a series can be used at the same time or one after another. Schoenberg said this way of looking at music is like looking at a hat from different angles — "Whether you see it from the front or sideways or upside down, you always recognize it as a hat." In July 1921, Schoenberg composed the Prelude of his Suite for Piano (1920–1923), his first piece based entirely on a twelve-tone note-row.

A LITTLE GOES A LONG WAY

Anton von Webern (1883–1945), a former pupil of Schoenberg, soon found a way to harness the twelve-tone method to his own, much sparer musical style. The result was a sequence of concentrated, atmospheric works, including his Symphony for Small Orchestra (1928), miniature Concerto (1934), and several sets of songs.

MOSES AND AARON

The twelve-tone method risks being dry and complex, but a great composer can produce masterpieces with it. Although Schoenberg never composed the third act of his opera *Moses and Aaron* (1932), the first two acts work well by themselves. The music has tremendous dramatic power. At first, this opera was thought too difficult to sing and play, so it was not performed until 1954.

A sculpture of Moses by Michelangelo (1475–1564)

BERG AND OPERA

Alban Berg (1885–1935), like Anton von Webern, was a former pupil of Schoenberg, but his musical personality was very different from Schoenberg's or Webern's. Berg adapted the radical technical ideas of Schoenberg and Webern to suit his own style, which was more directly related to the Romantic tradition of Austrian composer Gustav Mahler (1860–1911).

STORY OF AN UNDERDOG

The play *Woyzeck*, by 19th-century German writer Georg Büchner, was an almost unknown work about a poor, simple-minded soldier, struggling to support his girlfriend and their baby son. When his girlfriend is unfaithful, the soldier, Woyzeck, kills her, then kills himself. Berg was riveted by *Woyzeck*, when he saw it in Vienna, so he wrote an opera based on it, changing the soldier's name to Wozzeck.

Berg composed only a small number of works, but almost all of them are large-scale and richly detailed. His Chamber Concerto (1925) is an example.

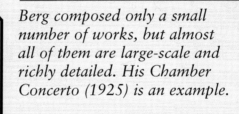

Berg dedicated Wozzeck to Gustav Mahler's young widow, Alma, who was a strong supporter of the Schoenberg school of composers. Alma Mahler later married the famous architect Walter Gropius.

Wozzeck was performed regularly during Berg's lifetime. When Berg died, Schoenberg wrote to Webern, "The saddest aspect is — it had to be the one of us who had success."

Panorama vom Wörthersee und Umgebung aus der Vogelschau.

Berg often composed at his Waldhaus, or forest house, near the Wörthersee lake in southern Austria.

BERG'S VIOLIN CONCERTO

Berg dedicated his Violin Concerto (1935) "to the memory of an angel." The "angel" was Manon Gropius. Manon was the daughter of Berg's friend Alma Mahler, widow of Gustav Mahler, and Walter Gropius. Manon died suddenly, and Berg's concerto reflects on her life, death, and memory. Before he could hear it performed, however, Berg himself died of a blood infection.

A WORLD-FAMOUS MODERNIST COMPOSER

In 1925, *Wozzeck*'s premiere in Berlin made a huge impact, in spite of an abusive newspaper review that objected to its dissonant modern score by "Alban Berg, a Chinaman from Vienna." The story is told in tightly constructed and intercut scenes, influenced by the techniques of the movies of the time. Berg's music strikes a balance between tonal and atonal music and draws together elements of both, creating a new and exciting style.

THE SEAMIER SIDE OF LIFE

Berg began *Lulu*, his second and last opera, in 1929, but he did not live to finish it. Based on two plays by German playwright Frank Wedekind, *Lulu* traces the path of a *femme fatale* and her various destructive relationships. Lulu is eventually murdered in London by the notorious Jack-the-Ripper. A version of Schoenberg's twelve-tone method is one of many technical devices Berg used in this opera. After Berg's widow died in 1976, *Lulu* was completed by Viennese composer Friedrich Cerha (*b.* 1926).

Manon Gropius died of polio when she was only eighteen years old.

FOLK SOUNDS

Before World War I, Hungary's Béla Bartók (1881–1945) and Czechoslovakia's Leos Janáček (1854–1928) were enthusiastic collectors of the folk music of central Europe. By the 1920s and 1930s, both of these composers had found ways to use folk styles in their music.

Throughout his life, Bartók wrote down the folk music he recorded in Hungary's villages and countrysides and often arranged it for the piano.

Bartók greatly admired the inventiveness and energy of Hungarian and Transylvanian folk music.

MODERNIZING FOLK DANCE MUSIC

For Bartók, folk music was ancient and timeless, yet also vividly alive. He felt it could fuel the development of genuinely modern music. In a sequence of string quartets and piano works, he forged a dissonant, driving, and exotic musical style, often built out of the melodic fragments that are typical of folk songs and dance music.

HUNGARY SINGS

Another Hungarian, Zoltán Kodály (1882–1967), responded to folk music in a style that was easygoing, straightforward, and colorful. Kodály's comic opera *Háry János* (1926), about a much-

10

Many Czechs resented Russia's powerful presence, but Janáček deeply admired Russian culture. His opera Katya Kabanova was based on a play by Russian writer Alexander Ostrovsky.

Janáček had to wait many years for international success, but he was proud of it when it came. In England, Janáček met conductor Sir Henry Wood (left) and was invited to Wood's country home near London.

loved rogue of Hungarian legend, was a great success. So were his orchestral *Peacock Variations* (1939). Kodály's *Psalmus Hungaricus* (1923), written for chorus and orchestra, is considered a proud, national masterpiece.

A LATE LOVE

As an old man, Janáček was swept up in a growing, yet mostly distant, passion for Kamila Stösslová, a younger, married woman. She inspired him to write music of blazing intensity that was rooted in the style of Czech folk music. These works include a sequence of great operas: *Katya Kabanova* (1921); *The Cunning Little Vixen* (1924), also known as *Vixen Sharp-Ears*; *The Makropoulos Case* (1926); and *From the House of the Dead* (1927). Other masterpieces by Janáček are his Sinfonietta (1926) for orchestra and his *Glagolitic Mass* (1926), a powerful choral setting of the Mass service in the old Czech language.

KAMILA STÖSSLOVÁ

"Today I have written down in musical notes my sweetest longings," wrote Janáček to Kamila Stösslová in February 1928. The music he had written was his Second String Quartet, which was published after his death with the subtitle *Intimate Letters*. Janáček himself called it "Love Letters."

Kamila Stösslová inspired Janáček's passionate Second String Quartet.

FROM GERMANY TO AMERICA

Germany's defeat in World War I led to the foundation of the Weimar Republic, named after the German town. The country suffered from poverty, high inflation, and mass unemployment under the peace terms of the victorious nations, Britain, France, and Italy. Life in Germany became very hard, and political extremism flourished. The result was the rise to power of Hitler and his National Socialist, or Nazi, Party in 1933.

Lotte Lenya was a singer and actress in both Weill's stage works and in films. She married Weill in 1926, but they divorced in the early 1930s.

MUSIC FROM HARD TIMES

Kurt Weill (1900–1950), the son of a Jewish cantor, caused a stir with his early Violin Concerto (1924). His style, influenced by both Schoenberg and Stravinsky, sounded more modern than any earlier music. Because Weill was sharply aware of the grim conditions around him in Germany, he wanted to reach more people, so he simplified his music to broaden its appeal. He also worked with Bertolt Brecht (1898–1956), a left-wing German playwright. Weill and Brecht wrote a sequence of theater works, including *The Threepenny Opera* (1928) and *Happy End* (1929), that revealed Weill as a great songwriter.

Among these posters is one proclaiming "Our last hope: Hitler." Another calls Nazism and Communism "enemies of democracy."

FROM BERLIN TO BROADWAY, VIA PARIS

In the 1930s, Weill collaborated with German writer Georg Kaiser (1878–1945) on the theater work *Silverlake* (1933). When Hitler's Nazis came to power and instantly banned *Silverlake*, Weill escaped from Germany and moved to Paris, where he met up again with Brecht and his then ex-wife, Lotte Lenya. Together they created *The Seven Deadly Sins* (1933), which mixes song and ballet. Weill and Lenya immigrated to the United States in 1935, where they remarried in 1936, and where Weill wrote his first Broadway shows, *Johnny Johnson* (1936) and *Knickerbocker Holiday* (1938).

MORE A HARDLINER

Like Weill, Hanns Eisler (1899–1962), who studied under Schoenberg, started out as an angry young modernist. His Marxist beliefs, however, led him to write music for audiences and performers outside middle class, classical concert halls, in places such as cabaret theaters, workers' choirs, and Berlin bars. In 1938, Eisler fled Hitler's Germany and moved to the United States.

When this photograph was taken in 1929, Kurt Weill's theater works were already famous throughout Europe.

COMPOSER WITH A CONSCIENCE

Paul Hindemith (1895–1963) felt that composers had a moral duty to widen classical music's place in society, so he wrote for students and amateurs as well as for professionals. His opera *Mathis der Maler*, or *Matthias the Painter*, (1934), about a medieval German artist's commitment to his work in a hostile world, was banned in Germany. It was first performed in Switzerland, in 1938.

Hindemith was also a violist.

13

Composer Weill and playwright Brecht argued sometimes, but, in general, they collaborated brilliantly. These pictures were taken in Berlin, in 1928, between rehearsals for the premiere of The Threepenny Opera.

STRAVINSKY AND NEOCLASSICISM

STRAVINSKY AND NEOCLASSICISM With World War I over, Paris once again became a magnet for artists from around the world. The international music scene in this colorful French city was dominated by composer Igor Stravinsky (1882–1971). Exiled from his native Russia, Stravinsky started a new life in France in 1920.

DANCING ON

The ballet *Pulcinella* (1920) was the first of Stravinsky's rediscoveries of the musical past. It was commissioned by his pre-war colleague, Russian impresario Sergei Diaghilev (1872–1929). *Pulcinella* adapts music by 18th-century Italian composers, such as Giovanni Pergolesi (1710–1736), in a brilliantly individual way. Its style, known as "neoclassical," is both distant and expressive. Stravinsky produced more ballet masterpieces with *Apollon Musagète*, or *Apollo, Leader of the Muses*, (1928) and *Perséphone* (1933), in which the principal dancer also narrates the story from ancient Greece. Stravinsky's *Symphony of Psalms* (1930), for chorus and orchestra, is another of his greatest works.

STRAVINSKY AND COLLEAGUES

Stravinsky was among the most famous classical composers of his day. He also traveled far and wide as a concert pianist. Living in Paris, he knew many of the world's great artists, such as painter Pablo Picasso. Because he composed so often for the theater, he became personal friends with writers, such as Jean Cocteau. He also knew many other musicians and conductors living or working in Paris.

Stravinsky (second from right) *in 1926 with* (from far left) *Cocteau, Picasso, and Olga Picasso, Picasso's wife*

14

CHILDHOOD AND JAZZ

Maurice Ravel (1875–1937) also produced some of his finest music in Paris after World War I. *L'Enfant et les Sortilèges*, or *The Child and the Sprites*, (1925) is a one-act opera about a naughty child who learns, from fairy-tale characters and the animals in his parents' garden, how to behave better. The opera uses the sounds of folk drumming and 1920s dances. Ravel's orchestral *Boléro* (1928), which was influenced by jazz and Spanish dance rhythms, became an instant classic.

Czechoslovakia's Bohuslav Martinu (1890–1959) went to live in Paris in 1923. There, he wrote music that was often about Czech subjects, such as his Field Mass *(1939). He also flirted with jazz and neoclassicism.*

For artists from all over Europe and America, Paris was the place to be. Writers Ernest Hemingway and James Joyce, as well as painter and sculptor Pablo Picasso, all lived there for a while.

The popularity in Paris of everything Russian continued after the war. Stravinsky's Mavra *(1922) and his opera-oratorio* Oedipus Rex *(1927) both premiered there.*

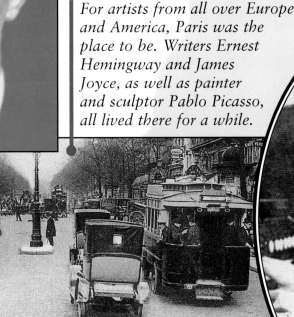

SACRED SOUNDS

In 1928, Olivier Messiaen (1908–1992) attracted attention with a short organ work, *Le Banquet Céleste,* or *The Celestial Banquet.* Its rich sound and religious theme were striking. His next works included a set of piano Préludes (1929), the orchestral *L'Ascension* (1933), and the organ cycle *La Nativité du Seigneur,* or *The Nativity of Our Lord,* (1935).

Olivier Messiaen played the organ at Mass every Sunday at the Church of Sainte-Trinité in Paris.

GREAT CONSERVATIVES

Some composers react less to the musical world around them as they grow older. Critics often accuse them of living in the past, saying their later works are the music of a bygone age. In fact, these later works enrich the musical world in their own ways.

Richard Strauss is pictured here with his wife, Pauline, a gifted soprano singer, and their young son, Franz. When not working hard at his music, Strauss enjoyed playing cards.

THE LANDSCAPE STILL SPEAKS

Already a star in his native Finland, Jean Sibelius (1865–1957) also became an international celebrity. As he grew more famous, however, Sibelius found it harder to create works that lived up to audience expectations. His Sixth Symphony (1923) and his Seventh Symphony (1924) were among his last and greatest achievements. He also wrote the magnificent symphonic poem *Tapiola* (1926), depicting Finland's forested landscapes. Sibelius almost certainly completed an eighth symphony, but, tortured by self-doubt, destroyed it.

This picture of Sibelius (standing, second from right) with Sweden's Wilhelm Stenhammar (1871–1927) (seated, far left) *and Denmark's Carl Nielsen (seated, far right)* was taken at the Nordic Music Festival.

OPERAS AND MORE OPERAS

Richard Strauss (1864–1949) started out as a radical young composer. Later, while living in the Bavarian mountains, he preferred composing in a masterly, conservative style. He wrote a long sequence of operas that included *Intermezzo* (1924), about a quarrel between himself and his wife; *Arabella* (1929), which was set in 19th-century Vienna; and *Daphne* (1938), a story from ancient Greece. Throughout his life, Strauss got involved as little as possible in the political and social upheavals going on around him in Germany.

A RUSSIAN EXILE

Having left his homeland after the 1917 revolution, Russian composer Sergei Rachmaninov (1873–1943) never returned. He lived mainly in New York and Switzerland, and he toured the United States and Europe as a concert pianist. Rachmaninov composed only six works in his later years, but all were important. Among them were the brilliant *Rhapsody on a Theme of Paganini* (1934), a Third Symphony (1936), and his *Symphonic Dances* (1940).

Gabriel Fauré (1845–1924) retired from teaching music in his old age, but he continued to compose it. Among his beautiful late chamber works are a Piano Trio (1923) and a String Quartet (1924).

With the earnings from his earlier operas, Puccini built a country home at Torre del Lago in Tuscany. Whenever he was composing there, he always wore a hat!

TURANDOT

In his later years, Giacomo Puccini (1858–1924) decided that his earlier operas were no more than *un burletta*, or a pantomime. He then set about composing *Turandot*, based on a Chinese legend about a cold-hearted princess who eventually yields to love. Although Puccini died before finishing the closing scene, this opera is his grandest, greatest, and most colorful work. It was completed by Italian composer Franco Alfano (1875–1954).

An illustration from 1926

LOCAL COLOR

Music around the world proudly reflected nationalist feelings. Composers in countries as far apart as Brazil and Poland aimed to create national styles that would have the strength and quality to be successful abroad.

DENMARK'S MUSICAL VOICE

Like Jean Sibelius, Denmark's Carl Nielsen (1865–1931) was a leading Nordic composer. Although Nielsen's lean, unexaggerated musical style was not directly based on folk music, it has come to be regarded as typically Danish. Among his most ambitious works is his Fifth Symphony (1922). His earlier cantata *Springtime on Funen* (1921) celebrated the Danish island where he was born. Nielsen also wrote chamber pieces, piano music, and songs.

Carl Nielsen's wife was a sculptress. By the time she made this marble portrait of her husband, Nielsen had risen from humble origins to international fame.

Szymanowski settled in Warsaw in 1919. He composed his first opera, Hagith, in 1922 and directed the Warsaw Conservatory of Music from 1927 to 1932. He died of tuberculosis in 1937.

Brazil's Villa-Lobos was so famous that the country put his image on some of its paper money.

BRAZILIAN CARNIVAL

Heitor Villa-Lobos (1887–1959) was a major Brazilian composer, who wrote over 2,000 works. After visiting Paris in the 1920s, Villa-Lobos returned to Rio de Janeiro, where he conducted, taught, and composed. His music combines the energy of Brazilian street bands with the methods of Western classical music. For example, his nine *Bachianas Brasileiras*, including one for soprano voice and eight cellos, blend Brazilian folk music with the technical devices of Bach.

POLISH ADVENTURES

Poland's Karol Szymanowski (1882–1937) visited Italy and north Africa. His travels inspired the unusual, exotic sounds in his early works. The opera *King Roger* (1926), set in medieval Sicily, explores the conflict between the King's Christian faith and the pagan influence of a mysterious, godlike visitor who came disguised as a shepherd. Szymanowski later became interested in the folk music of Poland's Tatra mountains. Its sounds and rhythms influenced his choral *Stabat Mater* (1926) and his ballet *Harnasie* (1935).

MANUEL DE FALLA

Two great inspirations for Manuel de Falla (1876–1946) were Spanish folk music and Spain's 16th-century golden age of classical music. In 1926, Falla started working on *Atlántida*, or *Atlantis*, a huge oratorio about Spain's destiny as the nation that discovered the Americas. He died before the oratorio was finished. A version was eventually completed by Spanish composer Ernesto Halffter (1905–1989), Falla's former pupil.

Falla (left) with Russian dancer Leonidé Massine on a visit to the Alhambra Palace in Granada, Spain

By the 1920s, Latin American dances, such as the tango, were popular all over the world.

JAZZ AND MUSICALS

America wanted to cheer itself up during the Great Depression, and Europe was determined to have fun after World War I. Jazz caught the mood of the times, and radio broadcasts and phonograph records brought it into almost every home. Meanwhile, on the silver screen, silent films were changing to "talkies," and musicals attracted huge new audiences.

Benny Goodman was one of the first to take jazz into the classical concert hall. In 1938, he played a legendary concert at New York City's Carnegie Hall.

AN ERA OF GREAT JAZZ ARTISTS

The piano playing of Jelly Roll Morton (1890–1941) was the talk of Chicago. Louis "Satchmo" Armstrong (1900–1971) mesmerized New York with his trumpet playing, singing, and scatting, the vocal technique he invented that used nonsense syllables to imitate instruments. Paul Whiteman (1890–1967) and Count Basie (1904–1984) guided jazz toward the 1930s big bands of clarinetist Benny Goodman (1909–1986) and trombonist Glenn Miller (1904–1944). Duke Ellington (1899–1974) expanded the scope of jazz numbers, paving the way for his trademark "symphonic jazz" as well as proving himself a sensitive and imaginative pianist. The sophisticated cornet of Bix Beiderbecke (1903–1931) pointed toward modern jazz, and the piano virtuosity of Art Tatum (1909–1956) amazed everyone.

When "Satchmo" moved from Chicago to New York, in 1924, his reputation as one of the greatest jazz trumpet players grew.

Show Boat opened in New York in 1927. The next year, bass singer Paul Robeson (1898–1976) appeared in its London premiere, singing "Ol' Man River."

20

EUROPE JOINS IN

In England, jazz influenced *Façade* (1922), an "entertainment" for reciter and instruments by William Walton (1902–1983). In France, Maurice Ravel (1875–1937) imitated jazz sounds in his two Piano Concertos (1930 and 1931). In 1934, jazz violinist Stéphane Grappelli (1908–1997) and guitarist Django Reinhardt (1910–1953) founded the famous jazz group Quintette du Hot Club de France.

THE BROADWAY MUSICAL LIGHTS UP THE WORLD

With *Show Boat* (1927), a rich spectacle of story, song, and dance, Jerome Kern (1885–1945) and Oscar Hammerstein II (1895–1960) produced a classic musical. Later, the music and lyrics of Cole Porter (1891–1964) sparkled in *The Gay Divorcée* (1932) and *Anything Goes* (1934). Hollywood quickly lavished its resources on movie musicals. *Show Boat* was first filmed in 1929, then the songs of Irving Berlin (1888–1989) graced the films *Top Hat* (1935) and *Follow the Fleet* (1936). George Gershwin, a master of the Broadway show, produced the wild score for *Shall We Dance?* (1937).

AL JOLSON AS *THE JAZZ SINGER*

Born Asa Yoelsen in Lithuania, Al Jolson (1885–1950) wowed Broadway audiences of the 1920s with his stage presence and his trademark phrase, "You ain't heard nothin' yet!" In 1927, when Warner Brothers made one of its first "talkie" movies, *The Jazz Singer*, Jolson starred in the title role. *The Jazz Singer* was a huge success, and the era of movie musicals was born.

21

Al Jolson moved successfully from stage to screen.

From 1927, Duke Ellington's fame as a pianist, composer, and arranger grew through his band's broadcasts from the Cotton Club in New York City.

AMERICA AND *AMERICAS*

Fired up by the excitement of the jazz age, American music brought fresh life and energy to the classical tradition. The genius and originality of George Gershwin (1899–1937), in particular, more than just crossed the boundaries between popular and classical music. His achievements greatly enriched both worlds.

SONGS, SHOWS, AND OPERA

Gershwin grew up listening to classical music, as well as to popular songs and jazz. In 1919, he wrote "Swanee," his first hit song. Many more songs followed, including "The Man I Love," featuring lyrics by his brother Ira (1896–1983). Gershwin's success extended to the Broadway theaters of New York with shows such as *Lady, Be Good!* (1924), *Oh, Kay!* (1926), *Strike Up the Band* (1927), and *Girl Crazy* (1930).

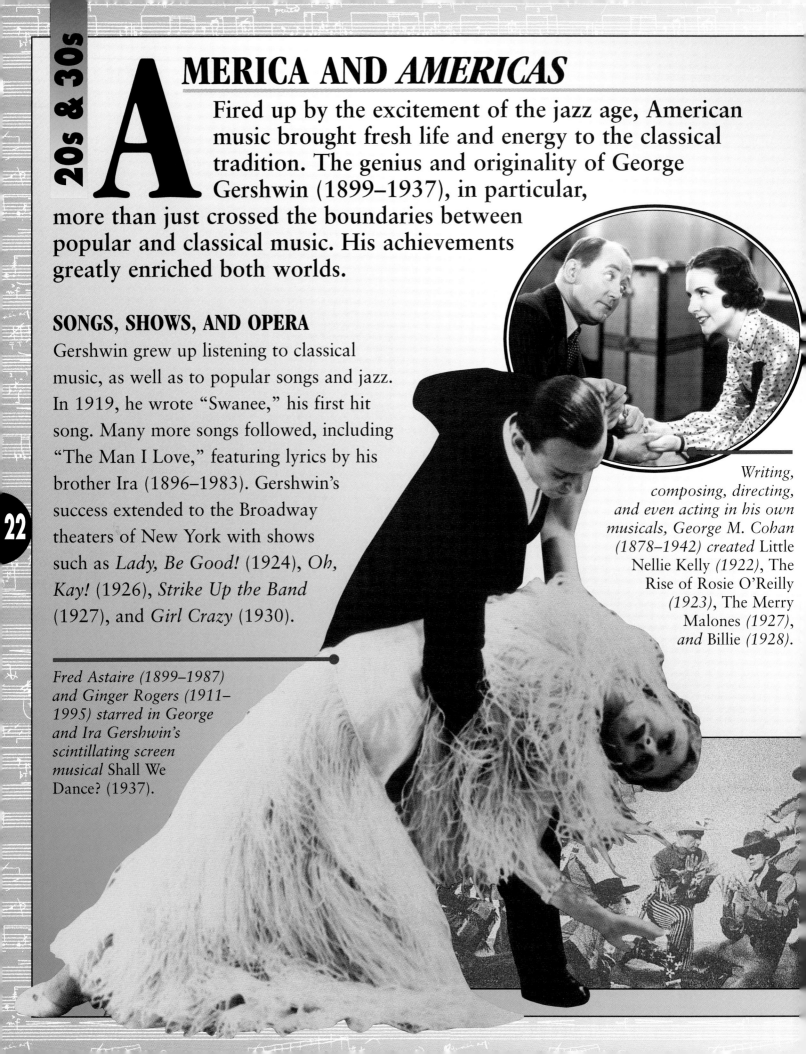

Writing, composing, directing, and even acting in his own musicals, George M. Cohan (1878–1942) created Little Nellie Kelly *(1922),* The Rise of Rosie O'Reilly *(1923),* The Merry Malones *(1927), and* Billie *(1928).*

Fred Astaire (1899–1987) and Ginger Rogers (1911–1995) starred in George and Ira Gershwin's scintillating screen musical Shall We Dance? *(1937).*

Gershwin dazzled audiences with *Rhapsody in Blue* (1924), a piece for piano and jazz band or orchestra commissioned by Paul Whiteman, and with Piano Concerto (1925). With *Porgy and Bess* (1935), he created a great American opera. Among the songs performed by its African-American cast are "It Ain't Necessarily So" and "Summertime." Tragically, Gershwin died from a brain tumor when he was only in his thirties.

FROM JAZZ TO THE PRAIRIE

Both Gershwin and Aaron Copland (1900–1990) were born in New York to Russian Jewish parents and both wrote in classical as well as popular styles. Copland's Piano Concerto (1926) contains jazz elements, while his Piano Variations (1930) are masterpieces of concise, "serious" style. *El Salón México* (1936), an orchestral piece, and *Billy the Kid* (1940), a ballet, were written for broad audiences.

MUSIC OF THE FUTURE

Edgar Varèse (1883–1965) moved from France to New York in 1915, hoping to discover new worlds of sound. He helped pioneer electronic music, and his dissonant *Amériques*, or *Americas*, (1921) even includes the sound of traffic sirens.

Billy the Kid *included cowboy songs, such as* "Git Along Little Dogie."

This Gershwin musical was a hit in 1927.

The brilliant collaboration of George (left) and Ira (right) Gershwin continued through Porgy and Bess, *in which the lyrics were cowritten by Ira and DuBose Heyward, and* Shall We Dance?

SOVIET RUSSIA

After the Russian Revolution of 1917, the Communist Party gradually increased its control of the country's culture. At first, composers were allowed to be radical and experimental, but when Joseph Stalin took over in the mid 1920s, this freedom was eliminated.

Although Lenin and his Bolshevik Party struggled at first to hold onto political power in Russia, they gradually took control of the Soviet Union.

THE MACHINE AGE

Revolutionary Russia was supposed to be leading its people into a new, industrial age of political and social equality. This official line was echoed in the heavy, pounding rhythms of *Steel* (1928), a ballet by Alexander Mosolov (1900–1973). The biggest star of the new Soviet Union, however, was Dmitri Shostakovich (1906–1975), who completed his First Symphony in 1925. It was soon played all over the world.

24

At just nineteen years old, Shostakovich (seated at the piano) penned a remarkably mature musical masterpiece. The young composer's First Symphony was one of musical history's most amazing debuts.

Composer Sergei Prokofiev (left) *and director Sergei Eisenstein worked closely together. At times, Eisenstein directed his filming to fit the music, rather than the other way around.*

PROKOFIEV'S ALEXANDER NEVSKY

In 1938, Russian director Sergei Eisenstein (1898–1948) directed the film *Alexander Nevsky*. Sergei Prokofiev composed one of the greatest of all musical scores for this film, which was a patriotic story about the winner of a battle on a frozen lake against an army of knights. Prokofiev subsequently reworked the music from the film as a cantata for chorus and orchestra.

Alexander Nevsky was a real-life Russian hero. The Russian Church declared him a saint in 1547.

SOVIET NIGHTMARE

In 1936, Stalin saw a performance of Shostakovich's new opera *Lady Macbeth of the Mtsensk District*. Disgusted by its story of adultery, murder, and suicide, and not appreciating the music's lurid brilliance, Stalin authorized a newspaper attack on Shostakovich. With political repression at its height, the composer feared for his life, so he withdrew both the opera and his Fourth Symphony (1936). The next year, his much less radical Fifth Symphony (1937) restored his official reputation. Although Shostakovich later revised his controversial opera as *Katerina Ismailova*, he wrote no new operas.

THE WANDERER RETURNS

Composer-pianist Sergei Prokofiev (1891–1953) had been living in exile in Europe and America. His return to his homeland in 1936, however, was badly timed. Soviet authorities wanted music about "Socialist realism," and they disliked the radical side of Prokofiev's style. Still, he scored hits with his children's entertainment *Peter and the Wolf* (1936) and his ballet *Romeo and Juliet* (1938).

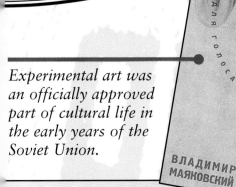

ВЛАДИМИР МАЯКОВСКИЙ

Experimental art was an officially approved part of cultural life in the early years of the Soviet Union.

BRITAIN AND BRITTEN

During the 1920s and 1930s, English music was looking both backward and forward. Ralph Vaughan Williams (1872–1958) was building on his earlier work with English folk songs. Benjamin Britten (1913–1976), a rising new star, was eagerly spreading his musical wings.

MORE THAN JUST A DREAM OF ENGLAND

Ralph Vaughan Williams served in the army in World War I. In 1921, he composed two deeply felt masterpieces that seemed to quietly remember the millions who died. They were *A Pastoral Symphony*, which he said was "not really lambkins frisking at all," and *The Shepherds of the Delectable Mountains*, a chamber opera. Some of his other works were *Job* (1931), a ballet based on the biblical story, and *Serenade to Music* (1938), written for sixteen singers and an orchestra.

In his cantata Our Hunting Fathers (1936), *Britten* (right) *set the poetry of W. H. Auden to music.*

The musical range of Ralph Vaughan Williams, who lived in London, was much greater than his false image as a country dweller suggested. His unaccompanied Mass in G minor (1921) is modeled on 16th-century English music, while his Fourth Symphony (1935) is full of dissonance.

THE NEW GENERATION

After causing early excitement with *Façade* (1922), William Walton (1902–1983) made a name for himself with his Viola Concerto (1929), the oratorio *Belshazzar's Feast* (1931), his First Symphony (1935), and his Violin Concerto (1939). Walton's music blended his own style of English lyrical beauty with snappy, driving rhythms. Michael Tippett (1905–1998) came to prominence with his elegant and lively Concerto for Double String Orchestra (1939).

A SPECTACULAR TALENT

Britten's tight-reined, but approachable, musical style combined a fluent composing technique with a boldly original perspective. He had early success with the *Variations on a Theme of Frank Bridge* (1937), for string orchestra, which was a tribute to the English composer who had taught him. Because Britten was a lifelong pacifist, he left England for America when World War II loomed. In America, in 1939, he composed his darkly troubled Violin Concerto and *Les Illuminations*, a vivid, brilliant song cycle that set the words of French poet Arthur Rimbaud (1854–1991) to music.

Jascha Heifetz (1901–1987) requested a violin concerto from Walton, who finished a lyrical and colorful masterpiece for this great American violinist in 1939.

ELGAR AT ABBEY ROAD STUDIOS

After the death of his wife in 1920, Edward Elgar (1857–1934) did not complete another major work. Instead, he conducted recordings of his earlier music, including his Violin Concerto (1910), featuring sixteen-year-old violinist Yehudi Menuhin. Elgar sketched out parts of a planned Third Symphony, but he never wrote it. In 1997, his plans were developed into a complete work by composer Anthony Payne (*b.* 1936).

Elgar conducted at the 1931 opening of London's legendary Abbey Road recording studios. Irish writer George Bernard Shaw (with white beard) is sitting below Elgar.

COMPOSERS REACT TO FASCISM

Some composers approved of the rise of extreme right-wing fascist power in Germany and Italy. Some did not, but felt they should stay and support their country's cultural values. Others left — in protest, out of fear for their lives, or both.

A MIXED RESPONSE

Italian composer Pietro Mascagni (1863–1945), who was famous for his opera *Cavalleria Rusticana*, or *Rustic Chivalry*, (1889) admired Italy's dictator Benito Mussolini. Mascagni composed the opera *Nerone* (1935) in Mussolini's honor. Other Italian composers, including Ottorino Respighi (1879–1936), Alfredo Casella (1883–1947), and Gian Francesco Malipiero (1882–1973), were mainly interested in their country's musical past, although Respighi's symphonic poems, *The Pines of Rome* (1924) and *Roman Festivals* (1924), share some of fascism's pride in the nation's past.

The 1936 Olympics in Germany featured music by Richard Strauss.

DEUTSCHLAND 1936
IV·OLYMPISCHE WINTERSPIELE
GARMISCH-PARTENKIRCHEN
6.-16. FEBRUAR 1936

Adolf Hitler seized on the German nationalism expressed in the operas of Richard Wagner (1813–1883). Here, Hitler is pictured at the Wagner Festival at Bayreuth with the composer's grandson, Wieland Wagner (right), and Wieland's English-born mother, Winifred Wagner.

Luigi Dallapiccola (1904–1975), who composed the modern opera *Volo di Notte*, or *Night Flight*, (1940) took a very strong antifascist position.

EXODUS

In March 1933, "serialist" composer Arnold Schoenberg was teaching at Berlin's Prussian Academy of Arts. When the Academy's director announced that Hitler was

Identifying with both Italian and German fascism, Pietro Mascagni (1863–1945) visited Berlin, where he composed his last opera, Nerone, in admiration of Mussolini. Other Italian musicians, at home and abroad, boycotted Mascagni's music.

Respighi's interest in his country's musical past influenced his dramatic cantata Lauda per la Natività del Signore, or Praise of Our Lord's Nativity (1930).

Luigi Dallapiccola's antifascist position meant that he had to live in hiding for many years.

THE 1936 OLYMPICS

The Nazi Party used the 1936 Olympic games, held in Germany, as an opportunity to promote its ideas about the superiority of Germany's white, "Aryan" race. The opening ceremony featured the choral work "Olympic Hymn," by Richard Strauss. While Strauss did not openly support the Nazis, he complied with official demands. He was an old man seeking a quiet life, and he had a Jewish daughter-in-law to protect.

determined "to break the Jewish stranglehold on Western music," Schoenberg stormed out. Soon after, he moved with his family to America. By 1940, Weill, Hindemith, Bartók, and Stravinsky had all joined him. Europe's loss was American music's gain.

"GOD BLESS AMERICA"

As fascism and the threat of war overtook Europe in the 1930s, Americans felt uneasy. In 1938, upon returning to New York from a visit to London, American songwriter Irving Berlin reworked "God Bless America," a song he had cut from an earlier show because it was too solemn. Berlin's new version of "God Bless America" was a soothing song for a troubled nation. Singer Kate Smith made it a hit, and the song continues to be popular, especially during difficult times.

TIME LINE

	WORLD EVENTS	MUSICAL EVENTS	THE ARTS	FAMOUS MUSICIANS	MUSICAL WORKS
1920	•U.S.: women over 21 get vote	•Duke Ellington leads various small bands	•Dadaism: anti-art Dada Fair held in Berlin	•Jazz saxophonist Charlie "Yardbird" Parker born	•Stravinsky: Pulcinella
1921	•Chinese communist party founded	•Schoenberg's first "serial" works	•Rudolf Valentino stars in The Sheik	•Death of composer Engelbert Humperdinck	•Prokofiev: The Love of Three Oranges
1922	•Russia becomes USSR	•Premiere of Janáček's Katya Kabanova	•James Joyce: Ulysses •T. S. Eliot: The Wasteland	•Jazz bassist Charles Mingus born	•Nielsen: Fifth Symphony
1923	•Italy: Mussolini seizes power	•Sibelius's Sixth Symphony performed	•W. B. Yeats wins Nobel Prize for Literature	•Death of composers Fauré and Puccini	•Stravinsky: Les Noces
1924	•Stalin takes power in the Soviet Union	•Schoenberg's Erwartung first performed	•E. M. Forster: Passage to India	•Louis Armstrong finds fame in New York	•Jean Sibelius: Seventh Symphony
1925	•Albania gains independence •Iran: Reza Khan is shah	•Premiere of Berg's opera Wozzeck in Berlin	•Sergei Eisenstein: The Battleship Potemkin	•Jazz vocalist Mel Torme born	•Alban Berg: Chamber Concerto
1926	•Britain: General Strike	•Première of Janáček's Glagolitic Mass	•Fritz Lang: Metropolis	•Jazz trumpeter Miles Davis born	•Sibelius: Tapiola •Show Boat
1927	•German stock market collapses	•Premiere of Stravinsky's Oedipus Rex	•First successful "talkie": The Jazz Singer	•American opera soprano Beverly Sills born	•Janáček: From the House of the Dead
1928	•USSR: Stalin's first five-year plan	•Weill and Brecht's The Threepenny Opera	•Walt Disney: first Mickey Mouse cartoon	•Cab Calloway leads the Alabamians jazz band	•Janáček: Intimate Letters
1929	•U.S.: Wall Street crash; Hoover elected president	•Film release of Show Boat	•First "true" musical: The Broadway Melody	•Jazz trumpeter Chet Baker born	•Walton: Viola Concerto •Webern: Quartet, op. 22
1930	•India: Gandhi leads Salt March protest	•Premiere of Gershwin's Girl Crazy on Broadway	•Greta Garbo makes her first talking movie	•Japanese composer Toru Takemitsu born	•Bartók: Cantata Profana
1931	•Japanese army occupies Chinese Manchuria	•Premiere of Shostakovich's The Bolt	•James Cagney stars in A Public Enemy	•Death of jazz cornetist Bix Beiderbecke	•Walton: Belshazzar's Feast
1932	•Nazis take control of Reichstag (parliament)	•Gershwin's The Gay Divorcée is staged	•Aldous Huxley: Brave New World	•Death of composer John Philip Sousa	•Schoenberg: Moses and Aaron
1933	•Hitler in power as Chancellor of Germany	•Louis Armstrong tours Europe	•Fay Wray stars in King Kong	•Schoenberg leaves Germany for America	•Stravinsky: Perséphone
1934	•China: Communists led by Mao on Long March	•Gershwin's Anything Goes is staged	•Henry Miller: Tropic of Cancer	•Death of composer Edward Elgar	•Vaughan Williams: Fourth Symphony
1935	•Italy invades Abyssinia (Ethiopia)	•Astaire and Rogers star in the musical Top Hat	•First Penguin paperback books	•Death of composer Alban Berg	•Gershwin: Porgy and Bess
1936	•Spanish Civil War begins •Edward VIII abdicates	•Prokofiev's Peter and the Wolf is a big hit	•Charlie Chaplin stars in Modern Times	•Composer Anthony Payne born	•Britten: Our Hunting Fathers
1937	•India: Congress Party wins elections	•NBC Symphony Orchestra created	•Picasso: Guernica •Walt Disney: Snow White	•Death of Ravel •Death of Gershwin	•Shostakovich: Fifth Symphony
1938	•Germany and Austria unite (Anschluss)	•Prokofiev's Romeo and Juliet first performed	•Orson Welles broadcasts The War of the Worlds	•Jazz trumpeter Freddie Hubbard born	•Webern: String Quartet, op. 28
1939	•Spanish Civil War ends •World War II begins		•Film release of Gone with the Wind	•Stravinsky moves to the United States	•Walton: Violin Concerto

GLOSSARY

atonal: the usually unstable and dissonant quality of music that is not written around a particular note.

cantata: a musical work composed for a chorus.

chamber music: instrumental music written for a small group of musicians, intended to be performed in a room or small concert hall.

chromatic: describing music that uses all twelve notes of the chromatic scale to form differing and sometimes extreme harmonies.

concerto: a musical work for a solo instrument and an orchestra, written in three different movements.

counterpoint: the technique of weaving together two or more different melodies.

dissonant: harsh sounding, as the sound produced by musical notes that are "unstable" when they are played together.

improvised: composed at the moment it is performed.

key: a group of notes, all related to a certain note, that defines the harmony of a piece of music.

neoclassical: newly made in a classical style.

oratorio: a musical work for solo voices, chorus, and orchestra, usually with a religious theme.

sinfonietta: a symphony written for a smaller than usual number of instruments.

string quartet: a musical work for four stringed instruments, usually two violins, a viola, and a cello.

suite: a collection of separate instrumental pieces.

symphonic poem: an orchestral work that tells a story or depicts a scene.

symphony: a long musical composition for a large orchestra, traditionally written in four movements.

MORE BOOKS TO READ

Count Basie. Black Americans of Achievement (series). Bud Kliment (Chelsea House)

Duke Ellington. Black Americans of Achievement (series). Ron Frankl (Chelsea House)

Introducing Gershwin. Introducing Composers (series). Roland Vernon (Chelsea House)

Introducing Stravinsky. Introducing Composers (series). Roland Vernon (Chelsea House)

Jazz and Its History. Masters of Music (series). Giuseppe Vigna (Barrons Juveniles)

Little Louis and the Jazz Band: The Story of Louis "Satchmo" Armstrong. Angela Shelf Medearis (Dutton Children's Books)

Movie Musicals. Silver Screen (series). Andrea Staskowski (Lerner)

The Random House Book of Opera Stories. Adèle Geras (Random House)

The Young Person's Guide to the Orchestra: Benjamin Britten's Composition. Anita Ganeri (Harcourt Brace)

WEB SITES

Ellington: The Shaping of a Hometown Legend. *www.pbs.org/ellingtonsdc/dukeEllington.htm*

Alban Berg. *www.geocities.com/al6an6erg/albanberg.html*

George Gershwin (1898–1937). *www.classical.net/music/comp.lst/gershwin.html*

Classical Music Pages: Béla Bartók (1881–1945). *w3.rz-berlin.mpg.de/cmp/bartok.html*

Due to the dynamic nature of the Internet, some web sites stay current longer than others. To find additional web sites, use a reliable search engine with one or more of the following keywords: *Irving Berlin, Britten, classical music, folk music, Gershwin, jazz, Carl Nielsen, opera, Arnold Schoenberg, Sibelius, Richard Strauss,* and *Igor Stravinsky.*

INDEX